¡L[illegible] el nuevo cachorrito!

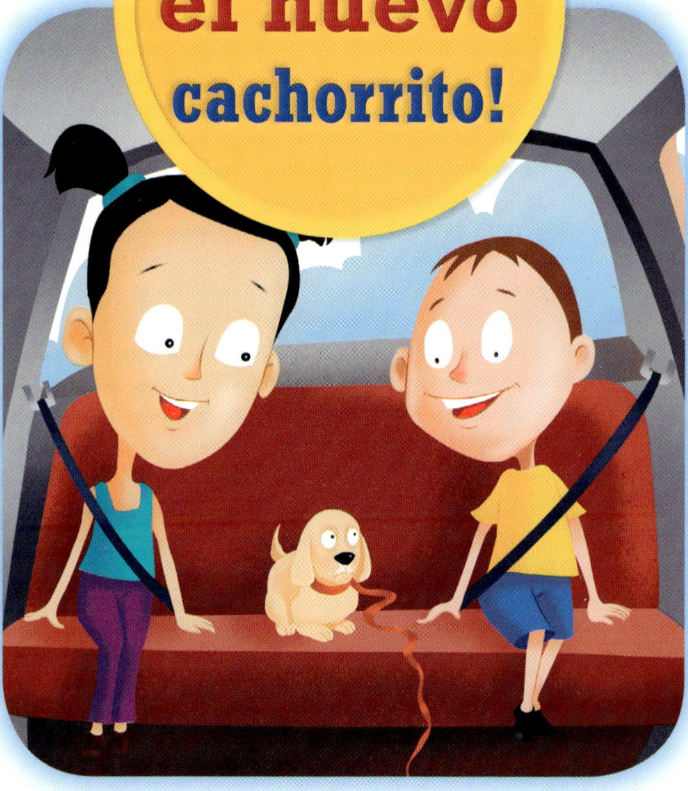

por Marcie Aboff
ilustrado por Nuri Vergara

Scott Foresman
is an imprint of

PEARSON

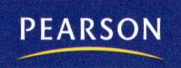

Glenview, Illinois • Boston, Massachusetts • Chandler, Arizona
Upper Saddle River, New Jersey

Every effort has been made to secure permission and provide appropriate credit for photographic material. The publisher deeply regrets any omission and pledges to correct errors called to its attention in subsequent editions.

Unless otherwise acknowledged, all photographs are the property of Pearson.

Photo locations denoted as follows: Top (T), Center (C), Bottom (B), Left (L), Right (R), Background (Bkgd)

Illustrations by Nuri Vergara

Photograph 8 Ariel Skelley/Getty Images

ISBN 13: 978-0-328-53322-0
ISBN 10:   0-328-53322-X

Copyright © by Pearson Education, Inc., or its affiliates. All rights reserved. Printed in the United States of America. This publication is protected by copyright, and permission should be obtained from the publisher prior to any prohibited reproduction, storage in a retrieval system, or transmission in any form or by any means, electronic, mechanical, photocopying, recording, or likewise. For information regarding permissions, write to Pearson Curriculum Rights & Permissions, One Lake Street, Upper Saddle River, New Jersey 07458.

Pearson® is a trademark, in the U.S. and/or other countries, of Pearson plc or its affiliates.

Scott Foresman® is a trademark, in the U.S. and/or other countries, of Pearson Education, Inc., or its affiliates.

1 2 3 4 5 6 7 8 9 10 V0G1 18 17 16 15 14 13 12 11 10 09

En el refugio viven animalitos.
Nos llevamos un perrito.
Se llama Ciro.

Ciro es un cachorrito muy bello.
Está un poco asustado.

Ciro necesita un tazón para el agua.
Necesita otro tazón para la comida.

Ciro va a la escuela para perros.
El maestro le dio una orden.
Ciro aprende a obedecer.

Ciro salió a jugar.
Conoció nuevos amigos.

Cachorritos

Leamos juntos

Cuando nacen, los cachorritos toman la leche de su mamá. Después de unas cinco semanas ya pueden comer. Tiene que ser comida para cachorritos, blandita y fácil de masticar. Los cachorritos sanos crecen más rápido. Necesitan comida, agua, ejercicio, siestas y mucho amor.